Excel for Writers

M.L. HUMPHREY

ISBN: 978-1-950902-41-5 and 978-1976508950

SELECT TITLES BY M.L. HUMPHREY

Affinity Publisher 1.0

Affinity Publisher for Book Formatting

Affinity Publisher for Ads and Covers

Affinity Publisher 2.0

Affinity Publisher for Book Formatting

Data Analysis for Self-Publishers

Writing for Beginners

Excel for Writers

Sell That Book

CONTENTS

Introduction

It probably has something to do with my background from before I started to write seriously, but I've always used Microsoft Excel to help me track and analyze my writing.

From the very first day, I've tracked my time spent on writing each day as well as my word count. And at the end of each year I've looked at key metrics to see if I'm writing more or less than in previous years and if my writing speed has improved or is holding steady.

When I started to submit short stories (when I was still on the trade publishing path), I tracked key information about the stories I wrote, the markets I submitted them to, and the results of those submissions.

When I finished the first draft of my first novel and realized it was horrible, I used Excel to analyze the chapters and viewpoint shifts to see what wasn't working.

And then of course were the moments when I wondered what it would really take to make a profit at this whole thing and I sat down to calculate what different levels of sales would net me.

(Always a scary calculation and one you probably shouldn't make if it will influence your decision to keep writing.)

All of this was done using Excel and it's what we're going to walk through in this guide.

Specifically, we will build worksheets that:

1. Track Time Spent Writing and Word Count
2. Compare Year-to-Year Writing Metrics
3. Project Potential Income Based on Trade Publishing a Novel
4. Calculate Short Story Income Based on Word Count and Pay-Per-Word
5. List Short Stories Completed
6. List Short Story Markets
7. Track Short Story Submission Results
8. Analyze Chapters and Scenes for a Novel
9. Track Character Names

I'm going to assume here that you know the basics of Excel already, so I'll focus instead on how to build each particular worksheet. This guide will be most useful to you if you build each of the worksheets as you go. Just reading this book will probably be a good sleep aid, but it won't teach you much.

If you're not familiar with a technique I mention, the appendices contain brief descriptions for every type of data input, formatting, and formula mentioned in this guide. I've capitalized the formatting and data input terms in the worksheet steps so you can easily cross-reference to the appendices.

The formulas are given to you and you just need to input them into the worksheet in the specified cell, but there is also a brief description of each formula used in Appendix C.

If you have no familiarity at all with Excel, the appendices will not be enough guidance for you. In that case, start with *Excel for Beginners* or some other basic Excel instruction guide first. But if you know the basics of Excel, you should be fine.

There are a couple more advanced uses of Excel, for example, Conditional Formatting, IF functions, and Pivot Tables, but I've walked through the specifics of how to use them in this context. (To learn more about those topics you can read *Intermediate Excel.*)

The worksheets discussed in this guide are designed to be used as-is. But what I would recommend is that you adapt them to your own personal needs and style. A lot of what this book is about is getting you to think about ways you can leverage this tremendous tool (Excel) to support your writing. So I'll also talk about how I personally use these reports and why I've structured things the way I have, but don't hesitate to make them your own.

Also, if you'd rather not go through the detailed work of creating each worksheet from scratch yourself, you can go to https://payhip.com/mlhumphrey and download the Excel for Writers Excel Template that was used to create the screenshots in this book for 99 cents. It will still need to be customized to you and your information, but using it may save you some time.

This guide is for any writer who wants to track their writing performance and do basic income calculations. If you're self-published, though, or planning to be, then I would suggest you also read, or read instead, *Data Analysis for Self-Publishers.*

Data Analysis for Self-Publishers covers topics like what information you should track, the importance of looking at profit and loss, visualizing your sales data, analyzing your ad spend versus your sales, calculating series sellthrough and customer value, and more.

One final point before we get started: This book was written using Excel 2013. Some of the ways of doing things described in the Appendices may not work quite the same way for you in whatever version of Excel you have, but the basics should remain the same no matter what version you have.

Okay, then. Let's get started with some baseline terminology and then we'll build the first worksheet.

Basic Terminology

Column

Excel uses columns and rows to display information. Columns run across the top of the worksheet and, unless you've done something funky with your settings, are identified using letters of the alphabet.

Row

Rows run down the side of the worksheet and are numbered starting at 1 and up to a very high number.

Cell

A cell is a combination of a column and row that is identified by the letter of the column it's in and the number of the row it's in. For example, Cell A1 is the cell in the first column and first row of a worksheet.

Click

If I tell you to click on something, that means to use your mouse (or trackpad) to move the arrow on the screen over to a specific location and left-click or right-click on the option. (See the next definition for the difference between left-click and right-click).

If you left-click, this selects the item. If you right-click, this generally creates a dropdown list of options to choose from. If I don't tell you which to do, left- or right-click, then left-click.

Left-Click/Right-Click

If you look at your mouse or your trackpad, you generally have two flat buttons to press. One is on the left side, one is on the right. If I say left-click that means to press down on the button on the left. If I say right-click that means press down on the button on the right. (If you're used to using Word or Excel you may already do this without even thinking about it. So, if that's the case then think of left-click as what you usually use to select text and right-click as what you use to see a menu of choices.)

Spreadsheet

I'll try to avoid using this term, but if I do use it, I'll mean your entire Excel file. It's a little confusing because it can sometimes also be used to mean a specific worksheet, which is why I'll try to avoid it as much as possible.

Worksheet

This is the term I'll use as much as possible. A worksheet is a combination of rows and columns that you can enter data in. When you open an Excel file, it opens to worksheet one.

Formula Bar

This is the long white bar at the top of the screen with the $f\chi$ symbol next to it.

Tab

I refer to the menu choices at the top of the screen (File, Home, Insert, Page Layout, Formulas, Data, Review, and View) as tabs. Note how they look like folder tabs from an old-time filing system when selected? That's why.

Data

I use data and information interchangeably. Whatever information you put into a worksheet is your data.

Select

If I tell you to "select" cells, that means to highlight them.

Arrow

If I say that you can "arrow" to something that just means to use the arrow keys to navigate from one cell to another.

A1:A25

If I'm going to reference a range of cells, I'll use the shorthand notation that Excel uses in its formulas. So, for example, A1:A25 will mean Cells A1 through A25. If you ever don't understand exactly what I'm referring to, you can type it into a cell in Excel using the = sign and see what cells Excel highlights.

=A1:A25

should highlight cells A1 through A25 and

=A1:B25

should highlight the cells in columns A and B and rows 1 through 25.

With Formulas Visible

Normally Excel doesn't show you the formula in a cell unless you click on that cell and then you only see the formula in the formula bar. But to help you see what I'm referring to, some of the screenshots in this guide will be provided with formulas visible. All this means is that I clicked on Show Formulas on the Formulas tab so that you could see what cells have formulas in them and what those formulas are.

Unless you do the same, your worksheet will not look like that. That's okay. Because you don't need to have your formulas visible unless you're troubleshooting something that isn't working.

Dialogue Box

I will sometimes reference a dialogue box. These are the boxes that occasionally pop up with additional options for you to choose from for that particular task. Usually I include a screen shot so you know what it should look like.

Paste Special – Values

I will sometimes suggest that you paste special-values. What this means is to paste your data using the Values option under Paste Options (the one with 123 on the clipboard). This will paste the values from the cells you copied without also bringing over any of the formulas that created those values.

Dropdown

I will occasionally refer to a dropdown or dropdown menu. This is generally a list of potential choices that you can select from. The existence of the list is indicated by an arrow next to the first available selection. I will occasionally refer to the list of options you see when you click on a dropdown arrow as the dropdown menu.

Capitalized Terms

One final note. There will be some weird capitalization in this document. That's because I've tried to capitalize each of the techniques that are covered in the appendices. So you might see a sentence that says: "Merge & Center and then Bold the text and add a gray Fill Color to the cell." If you know how to do all of that, just do it. But if not, if you go to the Appendices you will find entries for Merge and Center, Bolding Text, and Fill Color that tell you the basics of how to do each.

TRACKING YOUR TIME SPENT WRITING AND YOUR WORD COUNT

Now that we're on the same page in terms of terminology, let's get started with how to track your time spent writing and your word count for the day.

First, a little note about what I track and why. I track all of the time I spend writing and editing only. I don't track time spent on internet forums or tweaking my ads or loading files to various platforms or formatting ebooks or designing covers. Why? Mostly because that wasn't what I was initially doing and because it seemed to me that the core activity of being a writer is writing. I throw editing in there, too, because I'm one of those people that can go from a 60,000-word first draft to a 90,000-word second draft, so my editing time is often time spent creating new words.

I also, more because it's easy than anything else, only track my net word gain.

Huh? What does that mean?

It means I look at the word count on a document when I sit down to start writing/editing for the day and I compare that to the word count when I stop. It doesn't matter if I deleted 3,000 words and added 5,000, all I look at is the net change. In that case, the addition of 2,000 words. If I had an easy way of tracking new words, I might do so, but I don't, so I just track net words added and call it good.

You can choose to track whatever you want to track. The key is to not make it so complicated it gets in the way of what really counts, which is making progress with your writing. That's why the time tracking I do is very simple and only takes about a minute a day.

We'll start with the way I've been doing this for years, which involves using a day planner and then recording the results in Excel. And then we'll look at another way to do it that occurred to me while I was writing this guide where you track everything in Excel and use pivot tables to summarize your results.

Option 1: Using a Day Planner in Combination with Excel

Each year I buy a weekly planner with enough space for me to jot multiple notes on each day of the week. I need one that has enough space for all days of the week since I write most days of the week, and it needs to have enough room per day for me to have entries for up to five writing sessions. Each time I sit down to write/edit, I record what I'm working on, my start time, my stop time, and how many new words I added.

So today I have an entry that says, 2:10-3:10 Excel for Writers +742, meaning I worked from 2:10 to 3:10 on Excel for Writers and added 742 words to the file.

I keep doing this throughout the week and then at the end of the week transfer my totals for each day into my Excel file, which looks like this:

	A	B	C	D	E	F	G	H	I	J	K
1			Monday	Tuesday	Wednesday	Thursday	Friday	Saturday	Sunday		
2	7/3/2017	7/9/2017	0.25	1.5	2.5	3.5	0.5	0	1	9.25	
3	7/10/2017	7/16/2017								0	
4	7/17/2017	7/23/2017								0	
5	7/24/2017	7/30/2017								0	
6	7/31/2017	8/6/2017								0	
7	8/7/2017	8/13/2017								0	
8	8/14/2017	8/20/2017								0	

	L	M	N	O	P	Q	R	S	T	U
1			Monday	Tuesday	Wednesday	Thursday	Friday	Saturday	Sunday	
2	7/3/2017	7/9/2017	256	1850	3215	3600	50	0	1202	10173
3	7/10/2017	7/16/2017								0
4	7/17/2017	7/23/2017								0
5	7/24/2017	7/30/2017								0
6	7/31/2017	8/6/2017								0
7	8/7/2017	8/13/2017								0
8	8/14/2017	8/20/2017								0

As you can see, my Excel file has spaces for each day of the week across the top and a row for each week of the year. There's one section to track hours and one section to track word count. I also track the total for the week and the total for the year for each.

The view above is zoomed out so you can see both sections of the worksheet, but they're basically identical. I usually put the hours per day on the left-hand side and the words added on the right-hand side. You can do whatever works for you.

Here's just the time side of the tracker so you can see it easier:

	A	B	C	D	E	F	G	H	I	J
1			Monday	Tuesday	Wednesday	Thursday	Friday	Saturday	Sunday	
2	7/3/2017	7/9/2017	0.25	1.5	2.5	3.5	0.5	0	1	9.25
3	7/10/2017	7/16/2017								0
4	7/17/2017	7/23/2017								0
5	7/24/2017	7/30/2017								0
6	7/31/2017	8/6/2017								0
7	8/7/2017	8/13/2017								0
8	8/14/2017	8/20/2017								0

This is an incredibly easy worksheet to create. So let's do that. Remember, if you're not familiar with a technique, you can look it up in the appendices.

1. In Cells C1:I1, enter the days of the week. (You can use Auto Fill instead of typing each and every day of the week. See Appendix A.)
2. In Cell A2 type the date for the first day of the week you're starting with. In Cell B2 type the date for the last day of the week you're starting with. In my case that was 7/3/17 and 7/9/17.
3. Use Date Formatting to format Columns A and B.
4. In Cell A3 type the formula =A2+7

5. Copy the formula from Cell A3 into Cells A3:B53.
6. In Cell J2 type the formula =SUM(C2:I2)
7. Copy the formula from Cell J2 to Cells J3:J53.
8. In Cell J54 use AutoSum or type the formula =SUM(J2:J53) into the cell.
9. Copy Columns A through J and paste in Columns L through U.

That's it. You're done. If you want to get fancy you could insert a new Row 1 and Merge and Center the cells above each section and label them with "Writing/Editing Hours" and "Words Added" or something similar, but you don't need to unless you want to.

This format isn't fancy, but it gives me a nice visual of what I've written across a week and across a couple of months at a time. Be sure to also click into cell C2 and Freeze Panes so you can still see Row 1 when it gets to later in the year.

Here's the formula view for Columns A:J in case you need to see that:

	A	B	C	D	E	F	G	H	I	J
1			Monday	Tuesday	Wednesday	Thursday	Friday	Saturday	Sunday	
47	=A46+7	=B46+7								=SUM(C47:I47)
48	=A47+7	=B47+7								=SUM(C48:I48)
49	=A48+7	=B48+7								=SUM(C49:I49)
50	=A49+7	=B49+7								=SUM(C50:I50)
51	=A50+7	=B50+7								=SUM(C51:I51)
52	=A51+7	=B51+7								=SUM(C52:I52)
53	=A52+7	=B52+7								=SUM(C53:I53)
54										=SUM(J2:J53)

You'll note that I've scrolled down to the bottom here so you can see the formula in Cell J54, but remember that the date columns (A, B, L, and M) need to have a date entered in Row 2 for all of the subsequent formulas to work.

Also, what I sometimes do after using formulas to generate those dates in Columns A and B is Copy the columns and then Paste Special – Values in the same columns so that I'm left with the dates only. That way if I delete a row, I don't mess up all my dates. Just be sure to hit Esc or Enter after you do that. I can't count the number of times I used Paste Special-Values to remove formulas but somehow ended up with the formulas still there.

One final note. If you're crazy like I am and write across genres, you can create multiple worksheets like this, one for each type of writing you do, and then link them up to get your total hours and words written across all types.

I have a worksheet for novels, a worksheet for non-fiction, and a worksheet for short stories. I track each of those three separately and then have a final worksheet where the values in Cells C2:I53 and in Cells N2:T53 are actually formulas that pull from the other three worksheets. It's very simple to set up. Just do the formula once in Cell C2 and then copy to the other cells in the worksheet.

In my particular worksheet, the formula in Cell C3 is ='Novel Time Tracking'!C3+'Short Story Time Tracking'!C3+'Non Fiction Time Tracking'!C3. Your particular formula will depend on the name of each of your worksheets, but you can just click on each of the cells you want to include in your formula and Excel will figure that out for you.

Option 2: All in Excel Using Pivot Tables

Instead of my hybrid approach, you could, if you wanted, track all of the information directly in Excel. This has the advantage of letting you easily total hours by project, which is something my current approach does not do well. (I manually go back and track total hours once a project is finished.)

If you took this approach, your initial time tracking portion would look something like this:

	A	B	C	D	E	F	G	
1	Date	Start Time	End Time	Writing Time	Starting Wordcount	Ending Wordcount	New Words	Project
2	1-Jan	14:30	16:30	2.00	0	1500	1500	Project A
3	2-Jan	7:45	9:30	1.75	1500	1750	250	Project A
4	3-Jan	6:25	8:50	2.42	2250	2900	650	Project B
5	4-Jan	15:40	19:30	3.83	0	1000	1000	Project C
6	5-Jan	12:10	14:10	2.00	1750	2250	500	Project A
7	6-Jan	1:30	5:30	4.00	500	1250	750	Project C
8	7-Jan	13:30	17:45	4.25	1250	1600	350	Project C
9	8-Jan	11:00	13:20	2.33	2900	3600	700	Project B
10	9-Jan	12:10	14:10	2.00	1400	2500	1100	Project C
11	10-Jan	1:30	5:30	4.00	2500	3000	500	Project C
12	11-Jan	13:30	17:45	4.25	3600	5000	1400	Project B
13	12-Jan	13:30	17:45	4.25	5000	6500	1500	Project B
14	13-Jan	11:00	13:20	2.33	3000	4200	1200	Project C
15	14-Jan	12:10	14:10	2.00	2250	3750	1500	Project A
16	15-Jan	13:30	17:45	4.25	6500	8000	1500	Project B
17	16-Jan	13:30	17:45	4.25	4200	5000	800	Project C
18				49.92			15200	

You enter the date, your start time, your end time, your starting word count, your ending word count, and the project you're working on. Excel can calculate total time (Column D) and total new word count (Column G) using formulas.

This approach saves you having to transfer your information from a day planner to Excel and also saves having to calculate your time and word count change yourself.

So how to build it:

1. Label Cells A1:H1 as shown in the sample. (Date, Start Time, End Time, Writing Time, Starting Word Count, Ending Word Count, New Words, Project)
2. Add the following formula to Cell D2: =(C2-B2)*24

The reason you have to multiply by 24 is because Excel's default is to calculate the difference between two times in terms of how many days it is. So if you just take your ending time minus your starting time you'll get .04 for each hour you spent.

3. Add the following formula to Cell G2: =IF(F2>E2,F2-E2,0)

You need the IF function so you don't penalize yourself on days when you edit out words and don't add enough new words to have a net gain in word count.

4. Put a Border around Cells A1:H2.
5. Copy Row 2 down as many rows as you want.
6. Use Fill Color to add a color to Cells A1:H1. (I used blue for cells where I have to input information and gray for those where Excel will do the calculation for me.)
7. Bold the text in Cells A1:H1 and Wrap Text and/or adjust the Column Width so that each word falls on one line and is visible.
8. Use AutoSum at the bottom of Columns D and G to track your total hours spent writing and your total new words added.

There you have it. Nice and basic. Here's a picture of the worksheet with the formulas showing:

	A	B	C	D	E	F	G
1	Date	Start Time	End Time	Writing Time	Starting Wordcount	Ending Wordcount	New Words
2				=(C2-B2)*24			=IF(F2>E2,F2-E2,0)
3				=(C3-B3)*24			=IF(F3>E3,F3-E3,0)
4				=(C4-B4)*24			=IF(F4>E4,F4-E4,0)
5				=(C5-B5)*24			=IF(F5>E5,F5-E5,0)
6				=(C6-B6)*24			=IF(F6>E6,F6-E6,0)
7				=(C7-B7)*24			=IF(F7>E7,F7-E7,0)
8				=(C8-B8)*24			=IF(F8>E8,F8-E8,0)
9				=(C9-B9)*24			=IF(F9>E9,F9-E9,0)
10				=(C10-B10)*24			=IF(F10>E10,F10-E10,0)
11				=(C11-B11)*24			=IF(F11>E11,F11-E11,0)
12				=(C12-B12)*24			=IF(F12>E12,F12-E12,0)
13				=(C13-B13)*24			=IF(F13>E13,F13-E13,0)
14				=(C14-B14)*24			=IF(F14>E14,F14-E14,0)
15				=(C15-B15)*24			=IF(F15>E15,F15-E15,0)
16				=(C16-B16)*24			=IF(F16>E16,F16-E16,0)
17				=(C17-B17)*24			=IF(F17>E17,F17-E17,0)
18				=SUM(D2:D17)			=SUM(G2:G17)

One thing to realize about this worksheet is that you need to enter your times in military format. So, for any time from midnight to noon you would use 0-12 for your hours. But for your afternoon times, starting at 1 PM through 11 PM you'd use 13 to 23.

The only time this will really matter is if you work through one of those transitions. So if you put in 1:30-3:30 and you meant 1:30 in the afternoon to 3:30 in the afternoon, Excel won't care, it'll still calculate that as two hours either way. But if you put in 11:30-1:30, Excel will think you meant 11:30 in the morning and 1:30 in the morning on the same day and return a negative number. If you ever end up with a negative value, that's probably what happened.

Once you have your times and word counts entered, you can use pivot tables to generate a daily listing of total time spent and total words written.

To do so, highlight just your data. Don't include your summary line (Row 18 in this example). Go to the Insert tab, and choose Pivot Table.

I always choose to insert into a new worksheet, because pivot tables are dynamic and will change size and I don't want to risk overwriting my data. Putting it into a new worksheet will save you from that concern.

If you just want total hours per day and total words written per day, drag Date into the Rows section and Writing Time and New Words into the Values section to create your pivot table.

	A	B	C
1	Drop Report Filter Fields Here		
2			
3		Data	
4	Date	Sum of Writing Time	Sum of New Words
5	1-Jan	2	1500
6	2-Jan	2	250
7	3-Jan	2	650
8	4-Jan	4	1000
9	5-Jan	2	500
10	6-Jan	4	750
11	7-Jan	4	350

Be sure with your numbers in the Values section that it's taking a Sum of the values. Often with pivot tables mine will default to Count, and I have to click on the arrow at the end of the value description, choose Value Field Settings, and change it to Sum.

If instead you want to see total hours and words per project, you can just swap out Date with Project in the Rows section of the pivot table and you'll get something that looks like this:

	A	B	C
1			
2			
3		Data	
4	Project	Sum of Writing Time	Sum of New Words
5	Project A	8	3750
6	Project B	18	5750
7	Project C	25	5700
8	Grand Total	50	15200

The one thing this pivot table approach doesn't do as well as the other approach is give you a nice week-to-week view. But you can approximate it.

To do so, first add two columns to your original worksheet, one to specify which week of the year a date belongs to, and one to specify which day of the week it is. For Row 2, the first formula is =WEEKNUM(A2) and the second is =TEXT(A2,"dddd").

So with formulas visible and adding the two new columns as Columns B and C, we get:

	A	B	C	D	E	F	G	H	I	J
1	Date	Week	Day of Week	Start Time	End Time	Writing Time	Starting Wordcount	Ending Wordcount	New Words	Project
2		=WEEKNUM(A2)	=TEXT(A2,"dddd")			=(E2-D2)*24			=H2-G2	
3		=WEEKNUM(A3)	=TEXT(A3,"dddd")			=(E3-D3)*24			=H3-G3	
4		=WEEKNUM(A4)	=TEXT(A4,"dddd")			=(E4-D4)*24			=H4-G4	
5		=WEEKNUM(A5)	=TEXT(A5,"dddd")			=(E5-D5)*24			=H5-G5	
6		=WEEKNUM(A6)	=TEXT(A6,"dddd")			=(E6-D6)*24			=H6-G6	
7		=WEEKNUM(A7)	=TEXT(A7,"dddd")			=(E7-D7)*24			=H7-G7	
8		=WEEKNUM(A8)	=TEXT(A8,"dddd")			=(E8-D8)*24			=H8-G8	
9		=WEEKNUM(A9)	=TEXT(A9,"dddd")			=(E9-D9)*24			=H9-G9	
10		=WEEKNUM(A10)	=TEXT(A10,"dddd")			=(E10-D10)*24			=H10-G10	
11		=WEEKNUM(A11)	=TEXT(A11,"dddd")			=(E11-D11)*24			=H11-G11	
12		=WEEKNUM(A12)	=TEXT(A12,"dddd")			=(E12-D12)*24			=H12-G12	
13		=WEEKNUM(A13)	=TEXT(A13,"dddd")			=(E13-D13)*24			=H13-G13	
14		=WEEKNUM(A14)	=TEXT(A14,"dddd")			=(E14-D14)*24			=H14-G14	
15		=WEEKNUM(A15)	=TEXT(A15,"dddd")			=(E15-D15)*24			=H15-G15	
16		=WEEKNUM(A16)	=TEXT(A16,"dddd")			=(E16-D16)*24			=H16-G16	
17		=WEEKNUM(A17)	=TEXT(A17,"dddd")			=(E17-D17)*24			=H17-G17	
18						=SUM(F2:F17)			=SUM(I2:I17)	

We can then create a pivot table to replicate the grid in Option 1 (except with week numbers instead of date ranges). Like this:

Sum of Writing Time	Day of Week							
Week	Sunday	Monday	Tuesday	Wednesday	Thursday	Friday	Saturday	Grand Total
1	2	2	2	4	2	4	4	20
2	2	2	4	4	4	2	2	21
3	4	4						9
Grand Total	9	8	6	8	6	6	6	50

That's it. Two different ways for you to use Excel to track your daily and weekly hours spent writing/editing and words added to your works in progress.

Next, let's talk about a simple way to compare how you're doing year-to-year.

Year-To Year Tracking

Writing can be a hard slog. You set out all dewy-eyed with dreams of people oohing and aahing about that beautiful story you told, but it can take years to get to that point. It can even take years before you see a personalized rejection for a short story or get a full request when you query a novel.

So how do you keep yourself going in the meantime? How do you know that you're actually making progress?

What I do is track my writing numbers year-to-year using a very simple worksheet that looks like this:

	A	B	C	D	E	F
1		Year 1	Year 2	Year 3	Year 4	Year 5
2	Total Words	100,000				
3	Total Writing/Editing Hours	100				
4	Average Words (Week)	1,923	-	-	-	-
5	Average Hours (Week)	2	-	-	-	-
6	Max Words (Day)					
7	Max Words (Week)					
8	Words/Hour	1,000				

As you can see, I have one column for each year, and I track seven key pieces of information. Specifically, how many new words I wrote, how many hours I spent on writing and editing, how many average words I wrote per week, how many average hours I worked per week, the maximum number of words I wrote on any specific day, the maximum number of words I wrote during any specific week, and how many new words per hour of writing I averaged.

This gives me a nice snapshot of my efforts for a year. I can see if I wrote more this year than last year, if I picked up my speed, and if I became more efficient at my writing by increasing my average words per hour.

Sometimes I use these numbers to beat myself about the head for being a slacker. There was a year where I took on a work project that made me miserable and didn't write for six months straight. I assure you that when I got to the end of that year and looked at my numbers, I had some choice things to say to myself.

But don't do that.

Instead focus on how many total words you've now written and any improvements you've made.

So, how do you build this very simple worksheet?

1. Label Cells B1:G1 with Year 1, Year 2, Year 3, etc.
2. Label Cells A2:A8 with Total Words, Total Writing/Editing Hours, Average Words (Week), Average Hours (Week), Max Words (Day), Max Words (Week), Words/ Hour. (That's what I track, but if you want to track different metrics, list them here.)
3. In Cell B4 add the formula =B2/52
4. In Cell B5 add the formula =B3/52
5. In Cell B8 add the formula =IF(B3=0," ",B2/B3)
6. Copy Cells B2:B8 and paste them into Cells C2:G8

You should end up with a worksheet that looks like this (with formulas visible):

	A	B	C	D
1		Year 1	Year 2	Year 3
2	Total Words			
3	Total Writing/Editing Hours			
4	Average Words (Week)	=B2/52	=C2/52	=D2/52
5	Average Hours (Week)	=B3/52	=C3/52	=D3/52
6	Max Words (Day)			
7	Max Words (Week)			
8	Words/Hour	=IF(B3=0," ",B2/B3)	=IF(C3=0," ",C2/C3)	=IF(D3=0," ",D2/D3)

You may be wondering about the formula I had you use in Cell B8. Why did I have you use an IF function in that cell? Mostly because I don't like looking at #DIV/0! in a cell just because one of the cells used in the equation is currently blank. So what that IF formula is doing is saying, look, if cell B3, Total Writing/Editing Hours is empty, just leave this cell blank, too. If it's not empty, then divide total words by total hours.

Also, you should note that right now we have no values or calculations for Max Words. It's easy enough to find your maximums. The question is just whether you do so in your tracking worksheet and then manually record that value here or whether you do so straight from this worksheet.

Your choice. The formula you want is MAX( ).

So if we're using Option 1 above and I have all of my time tracking for the year in a worksheet called Word and Time Tracking and my word counts are tracked in Columns N through T, then the formula I'd want for Max Words (Day) is =MAX('Word and Time Tracking'!N2:T53) assuming we're in the same Excel file. What that formula is saying is take the maximum value from Cells N2 through T53 in the worksheet called Word and Time Tracking. In the same way, if I want Max Words (Week), the formula would be =MAX('Word and Time Tracking'!U2:U53) since Column U is where we total the daily values into a weekly value.

I tend not to do it this way. I instead calculate my maximums in the worksheet itself and then just copy over the numerical value into my year-to-year worksheet. That's because I track the numbers in separate files and don't want to run into an issue with Excel where it needs to update values and fails to find the source file. Once a number is locked down, I like to store it as a number instead of as a formula.

But that's me. And there are arguments to be made either way.

If you used Option 2 above and have a pivot table of words written per week and you want the maximum for any given day, there are a couple ways to do it.

You can highlight all of the cells in the table, right-click on the status bar at the bottom of the screen, and customize your Status Bar to include Maximum. You'll then see the maximum value of the highlighted cells displayed in the bottom right corner of your file and can enter it into your year-to-year worksheet.

Or you can use the MAX function on the daily values in the pivot table. Just input =MAX( ) into a cell in your worksheet with the cell range for the daily values in your pivot table inside the parens. So in our example below that would be =MAX(B5:H7).

If you do that, though, I would not recommend keeping that as a formula. As I mentioned before, pivot tables are dynamic so they can change their size as their data inputs change. You may never have an issue with it if you're done with that year and your data is stable, but if you ever refresh the table, you could break the formula. Better to get your value and type it into the cell in your year-to-year tracking table. You're only going to have to do this once a year, after all.

Both of the methods I just described can also be used to calculate your weekly maximum value. In addition, you can simply sort the Grand Total column in the pivot table in descending order. To do so, right-click in one of the cells under Grand Total and choose sort Largest to Smallest.

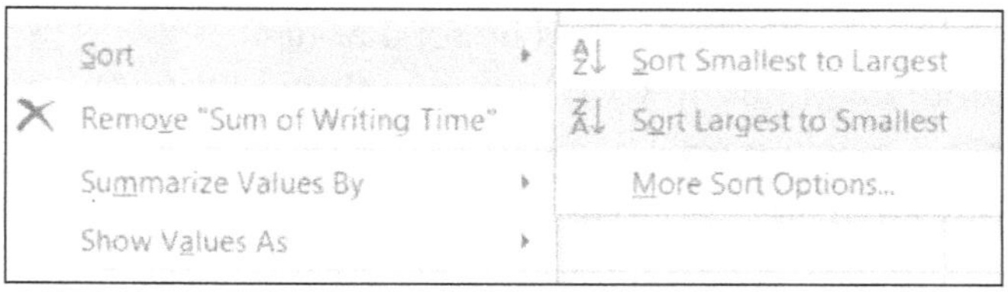

Income Projections

I'm a numbers person, so I can't help but calculate what I could potentially earn or what it will take me to get to a certain point income-wise. It's just something I have to do. But doing so can be demoralizing. So if you're one of those people who just doesn't want to know or think about this at all, skip to the next section.

And honestly, if you run the numbers on writing and let the average drive your decisions, you'll probably never get started. There's some statistic floating around out there about how the average novel only sells 200 copies. You don't have to be a rocket scientist to do the math on that number and know that isn't enough to pay your rent. And yet every year there are authors who break out. Authors who sell not just 200 copies or a thousand but ten thousand or a hundred thousand or a million copies. If the authors of Hunger Games or Twilight had crunched these numbers and let that drive their decisions, it's quite possible they'd be lawyers instead. I certainly know that if I want to make good money it's far more likely I could do so with my consulting work than with my writing.

So keep that in mind.

I still run the numbers though.

Example 1: Trade Publishing A Novel

Before we look at this specific example, you should understand that the reality is much more nuanced than what I have in this worksheet.

First, I'm not looking at advances at all, which is where most authors will earn most of their trade publishing income. (From what I've read, most authors don't earn out their advances, so the advance is actually all you get for most book deals.)

Second, I'm not accounting for deeply discounted sales. I'm assuming all sales in each category are going to be at full list price, which is probably not an accurate assumption.

Third, the percentages I'm using may not be what you get in your contract. You should change them to whatever you want them to be.

I'm also not including audio sales or foreign rights sales, which will probably come in lump sums like an advance would and can be a sizeable payment when they happen. (Can be. Not always.)

So, having said all that, here's what I put together when I was trying to judge trade publishing numbers:

	A	B	C	D	E	F	G	H	I	J	K	L	M	N	O	P
1	Assumptions	HC Price	Percent Pay			PB Price	Percent Pay			Ebook Price	Percent Pay				Agent Fee	Hours Per Novel
2		$25	10%			$8	6%			$10	30%				15%	300
4	HC Units Sold	Per Unit Gross	Total Gross		PB Units Sold	Per Unit Gross	Total Gross		Ebook Units Sold	Per Unit Gross	Total Gross		Total Units	Gross	Net After Pay Agent	Hourly Wage
5									50	$3.00	$149.85		50	$149.85	$127.37	$0.42
6									250	$3.00	$749.25		250	$749.25	$636.86	$2.12
7									500	$3.00	$1,498.50		500	$1,498.50	$1,273.73	$4.25
8									1,000	$3.00	$2,997.00		1,000	$2,997.00	$2,547.45	$8.49
10					50	$0.48	$24.00		150	$3.00	$449.55		200	$473.55	$402.52	$1.34
11					250	$0.48	$120.00		750	$3.00	$2,247.75		1,000	$2,367.75	$2,012.59	$6.71
12					500	$0.48	$240.00		1,500	$3.00	$4,495.50		2,000	$4,735.50	$4,025.18	$13.42
13					1000	$0.48	$480.00		3,000	$3.00	$8,991.00		4,000	$9,471.00	$8,050.35	$26.83
15	50	$2.50	$125.00		250	$0.48	$120.00		750	$3.00	$2,247.75		1,050	$2,492.75	$2,118.84	$7.06
16	100	$2.50	$250.00		500	$0.48	$240.00		1,500	$3.00	$4,495.50		2,100	$4,985.50	$4,237.68	$14.13
17	250	$2.50	$625.00		1,250	$0.48	$600.00		3,750	$3.00	$11,238.75		5,250	$12,463.75	$10,594.19	$35.31

Here's the left-hand side in closer detail:

	A	B	C	D	E	F	G
1	Assumptions	HC Price	Percent Pay			PB Price	Percent Pay
2		$25	10%			$8	6%
4	HC Units Sold	Per Unit Gross	Total Gross		PB Units Sold	Per Unit Gross	Total Gross
5							
6							
7							
8							
10					50	$0.48	$24.00
11					250	$0.48	$120.00
12					500	$0.48	$240.00
13					1000	$0.48	$480.00
15	50	$2.50	$125.00		250	$0.48	$120.00
16	100	$2.50	$250.00		500	$0.48	$240.00
17	250	$2.50	$625.00		1,250	$0.48	$600.00

Here's the right-hand side in closer detail:

I	J	K	L	M	N	O	P
	Ebook Price	Percent Pay				Agent Fee	Hours Per Novel
	$10	30%				15%	300
Ebook Units Sold	Per Unit Gross	Total Gross		Total Units	Gross	Net After Pay Agent	Hourly Wage
50	$3.00	$149.85		50	$149.85	$127.37	$0.42
250	$3.00	$749.25		250	$749.25	$636.86	$2.12
500	$3.00	$1,498.50		500	$1,498.50	$1,273.73	$4.25
1,000	$3.00	$2,997.00		1,000	$2,997.00	$2,547.45	$8.49
150	$3.00	$449.55		200	$473.55	$402.52	$1.34
750	$3.00	$2,247.75		1,000	$2,367.75	$2,012.59	$6.71
1,500	$3.00	$4,495.50		2,000	$4,735.50	$4,025.18	$13.42
3,000	$3.00	$8,991.00		4,000	$9,471.00	$8,050.35	$26.83
750	$3.00	$2,247.75		1,050	$2,492.75	$2,118.84	$7.06
1,500	$3.00	$4,495.50		2,100	$4,985.50	$4,237.68	$14.13
3,750	$3.00	$11,238.75		5,250	$12,463.75	$10,594.19	$35.31

Let's look at this for a second before we start to build it.

First, across the top we have our assumptions. There are eight of them. I had to decide what I thought hard covers, paperbacks, and ebooks would sell for and then what percentage of that sales price I'd receive. Next, I wanted to account for an agent's share of the earnings, and, finally, how long it would take me to produce a novel so I could figure out an hourly wage equivalent. If you think your numbers would be different, then use different numbers. Note also that I didn't account for any escalator clause where more copies sold means a higher percentage payout.

The next section includes the actual calculations of potential earnings. The first four lines are a scenario involving an ebook-only publisher. The next four lines of numbers are a scenario involving a book that's only published in mass-market paperback and ebook. The rest are a scenario where the book is published in hard cover, mass-market paperback, and ebook. (When I first did this worksheet, I assumed all deals would involve a hardcover, but that's definitely not the case for many authors, especially on their first deal.) I'm also assuming a mass market paperback here even though I've heard those deals are becoming less common. Feel free to change the paperback price to a trade paperback price instead. (Somewhere in the range of $15.)

Again, run the scenarios that make sense for your situation.

One thing that's hidden in this worksheet is that I assumed that paperback sales would be five times those of hardcover sales and that ebook sales would be three times paperback sales. You might want to make very different assumptions. I know for some of my self-published titles it would be more like ebook sales are ninety times paperback sales.

(All these assumptions are why in business school I realized that valuing a company is as much art as science and that you can pretty much come up with any number you want if you just change your assumptions. Now, whether that number is realistic or not…Well, that's another question entirely.)

Alright, then. Let's build this thing.

1. Label Cells A1:C1, F1:G1, J1:K1, and O1:P1. (Assumptions, HC Price, Percent Pay, PB Price, Percent Pay, Ebook Price, Percent Pay, Agent Fee, Hours Per Novel)
2. Add Borders around Cells B1:C2, F1:G2, J1:K2, and O1:P2.
3. Use Fill Color to fill Cells B1:C1, F1:G1, J1:K1, and O1:P1 with your chosen cell color.
4. Label Cells A4:P4. (HC Units Sold, Per Unit Gross, Total Gross, PB Units Sold, Per Unit Gross, Total Gross, Ebook Units Sold, Per Unit Gross, Total Gross, Total Units, Gross, Net After Pay Agent, Hourly Wage)
5. Place Borders around Cells A4:P5.
6. In Cell B5 add the formula =$C$2*$B$2

(Note that in the screenshot I've deleted the formula from Cells B5 through B14, but right now it's easier to include the formulas in row 5.)

7. In Cell F5 add the formula =$G$2*$F$2
8. In Cell J5 add the formula =$J$2*$K$2

(Note that all three of these formulas use $ signs because they are referencing the assumed values at the top of the worksheet and will stay the same across all of the rows.)

9. In Cell C5 add the formula =B5*A5
10. In Cell G5 add the formula =F5*E5
11. In Cell K5 add the formula =J5*I5
12. In Cell M5 add the formula =A5+E5+I5
13. In Cell N5 add the formula =C5+G5+K5
14. In Cell O5 add the formula =(1-$O$2)*N5
15. In Cell P5 add the formula =O5/$P$2
16. Copy Row 5 and Paste downward as many rows as you want.
17. Use Fill Color to fill cells A4:P4 with a cell color, preferably a different one from what you used for the assumption labels in Row 1.
18. If you want, change the Row Height of Row 3 and Insert Rows into your table and change their row height to match Row 3's height to separate different scenarios. Fill the cells in those inserted rows with a gray color. (Like Rows 9 and 14 in the sample worksheet.)

19. If you want, change the Column Widths of Columns D, H, and L.

    (You can use Ctrl to select all three at once and adjust them together or you can adjust one and then use the Format Painter to change the other two to match. Or you can just format them like you would a normal column.)

20. Add your assumed values to Cells B2, C2, F2, G2, J2, K2, O2, P2, and Columns A, E and I in your table.
21. Use Number Formatting on the cells in the table in Columns A, E, I and M to include a thousands separator and no decimal places.
22. Use Currency Formatting on the cells in the table in Columns B, C, F, G, J, K, N, O, and P to format them as currency.
23. If not already formatted that way when they were inputted, use Currency Formatting on cells B2, F2, and J2; Percent Formatting on cells C2, G2, K2, and O2; and Number Formatting on cell P2.

That should do it. It looks like a lot of steps, but most of those steps are about making it look good not making it functional. You don't have to use colors on your header rows or format your cells specific ways or change the height of your rows or the width of your columns. I just think it makes it more visually clear when you do.

This is what it should look like before you enter your assumptions and with formulas visible:

First Half:

	A	B	C	D	E	F	G
1	Assumptions	HC Price	Percent Pay			PB Price	Percent Pay
2							
4	HC Units Sold	Per Unit Gross	Total Gross		PB Units Sold	Per Unit Gross	Total Gross
5		=$C$2*$B$2	=B5*A5			=$G$2*$F$2	=F5*E5
6		=$C$2*$B$2	=B6*A6			=$G$2*$F$2	=F6*E6
7		=$C$2*$B$2	=B7*A7			=$G$2*$F$2	=F7*E7
8		=$C$2*$B$2	=B8*A8			=$G$2*$F$2	=F8*E8

Second Half:

	I	J	K	L	M	N	O	P
1		Ebook Price	Percent Pay				Agent Fee	Hours Per Novel
2								
4	Ebook Units Sold	Per Unit Gross	Total Gross		Total Units	Gross	Net After Pay Agent	Hourly Wage
5		=$J$2*$K$2	=J5*I5		=A5+E5+I5	=C5+G5+K5	=(1-$O$2)*N5	=O5/$P$2
6		=$J$2*$K$2	=J6*I6		=A6+E6+I6	=C6+G6+K6	=(1-$O$2)*N6	=O6/$P$2
7		=$J$2*$K$2	=J7*I7		=A7+E7+I7	=C7+G7+K7	=(1-$O$2)*N7	=O7/$P$2
8		=$J$2*$K$2	=J8*I8		=A8+E8+I8	=C8+G8+K8	=(1-$O$2)*N8	=O8/$P$2

Now let's move on to a short story scenario since that's how a lot of people start or break in, at least with speculative fiction.

Example 2: Selling a Short Story

I love building scenario tables where I look at the intersection between two separate variables. They're very easy to do and incredibly powerful. I do them for pairings like consulting rates and hours worked or sale price of my house and broker's commission. You can use a chart like this for any scenario where you have two variables and want to see what the results are when you change one or both of them.

In this case we're looking at what you might get paid for a short story depending on its word count and the pay rate for the market where you sell it.

Here it is. Nice and simple.

	A	B	C	D	E	F	G
1			**Pay Per Word**				
2			0.005	0.01	0.05	0.08	0.25
3	**Wordcount**	500	$2.50	$5.00	$25.00	$40.00	$125.00
4		1,000	$5.00	$10.00	$50.00	$80.00	$250.00
5		2,500	$12.50	$25.00	$125.00	$200.00	$625.00
6		5,000	$25.00	$50.00	$250.00	$400.00	$1,250.00
7		7,500	$37.50	$75.00	$375.00	$600.00	$1,875.00
8		10,000	$50.00	$100.00	$500.00	$800.00	$2,500.00
9		12,500	$62.50	$125.00	$625.00	$1,000.00	$3,125.00
10		15,000	$75.00	$150.00	$750.00	$1,200.00	$3,750.00

See what it's doing? You can look at any of the rows to see what you can earn for a given word count. Or you can look at any column to see what different word counts will earn you at that payout level.

Let's build it real quick and then we'll look at it again.

1. In Cell C1 type Pay Per Word.
2. Highlight Cells C1:G1 and choose to Merge and Center. Bold the text, change the cell color (with Fill Color), and add a Border around the edge.
3. In Cell A3 type Word Count.
4. Highlight Cells A3:A10 and choose to Merge and Center. Bold the text, change the cell color, and add a Border around the edge.
5. Change the Cell Text Orientation to 90 degrees and the Cell Text Alignment so that it's centered both horizontally and vertically.
6. Add values to Cells C2:G2 and B3:B10. Color the cells using Fill Color.

7. Format Cells B3:B10 using Number Formatting so that they use a thousands separator but no decimal places.
8. In Cell C3, type the following formula: =$B3*C$2
9. Copy the formula from Cell C3 to Cells C3:G10.

   (Note that this works because we used the $ signs in the original formula in Cell C3 to fix the references to Column B and Row 2 while allowing the row number with respect to Column B and the Column number with respect to Row 2 to change.)

10. Use Currency Formatting to format Cells C3:G10 as currency.
11. Put Borders around Cells B3:B10, and C2:G10.

That's it. Easy as. And now you can see that the difference between selling that 5,000-word short story to a token market that pays you half a cent per word and a high-paying pro market that pays you 25 cents per word is over $1,200. So always aim high. Start with the best markets and work your way down. The worst they can say is no. But if they say yes? You're $1,200 richer than you would've been if you'd started at the bottom.

Short Story Listing

If you're writing a lot of short stories and submitting them to markets, there's definitely a need to know what you've written in terms of genre and length so you can figure out where to submit.

What information you choose to track is up to you. Below is the worksheet I used to use:

	A	B	C	D	E	F	G	H	I	J	K	L
1	#	Title	Genre	Word Count	Date Started	Date Finished	Time Spent on Writing	Time to Review Reader Edits/ Final Proof	Time Spent on Submissions	Total Hours	Sold First Rights To	Amount Paid
2										0		
3										0		
4										0		
5										0		
6										0		
7										0		
8										0		

It's very basic and mostly just a summary of information about each short story. Namely, title, word count, when I started it, when I finished it, how much time I spent on it, and where it sold.

There's only one column in the entire document that has a formula in it. Column J, which adds up total time spent between writing, revising, and submitting.

What's nice with a document like this is that you can then filter your data and see, for example, only your fantasy short stories that are between 5,000 and 7,500 words.

And, when you do sell a story, it's a convenient location to record what you made from that story rather than having to dig through your bank or PayPal statements.

So, let's build it:

1. Label Cells A1:L1. (#, Title, Genre, Word Count, Date Started, Date Finished, Time Spent on Writing, Time to Review Reader Edits/Final Proof, Time Spent on Submissions, Total Hours, Sold First Rights To, Amount Paid)
2. Place a Border around Cells A1:L2.
3. Add a Fill Color to Cells A1:L1.
4. Format Cell D2 using Number Formatting to use a thousands separator and no decimal places.

5. Format Cells E2 and F2 using Date Formatting.
6. Format Cell L2 using Currency Formatting.
7. In Cell J2 add the formula =G2+H2+I2 or =SUM(G2:I2).
8. Copy Row 2 down as many rows as you want.

That's it. A nice, simple listing of everything you've written. Something you'll want to track for as long as you're a writer and maybe even after, especially if you sell your stories. You never know when someone might come looking for reprint rights, after all.

Next, we'll discuss a way to track available short story markets.

Short Story Market Listing

When I was regularly submitting to short story markets, I kept a worksheet that listed all speculative fiction markets I was interested in. That list included their pay rates at different word counts, what type of speculative fiction they accepted, and what their actual submission guidelines said.

You may not want to bother with this. There are websites that track short story markets for you that are nice and easy to use. One is Duotrope (https://duotrope.com/) although it's no longer free. Another, which is still free, is The Submission Grinder (https://thegrinder.diabolicalplots.com/).

Since the Grinder is free, I'll focus on that one. If you know the market you're looking for, you can go to the Grinder and search for that market. It will tell you what genres that market takes, how long your story needs to be, what they pay, what their acceptance rate is, and what the average response time is. If you're not sure what market you're looking for, you can search by genre, word count, payment, etc. The site also lets you create an account and track your submissions so you know what you've submitted where, how long it's been outstanding, and how that compares to others' experiences.

I used both of those sites when I was regularly submitting short stories. But I also found it helpful to keep a more detailed listing of information for the top markets I was submitting to, because there's always more nuance involved with payout and guidelines than a standardized form can capture.

For example, neither site notes what length preference a market has. They just state the overall range that's accepted. You can also tell a lot about a market based on how it phrases its guidelines. If you have a zombie story, there's at least one market out there you do not want to submit to because they very clearly do not like them.

Here's what I came up with:

First Half:

	A	B	C	D	E	F	G	H
1	**Name**	**Genre**	**Pay Rate**	**1,500**	**2,500**	**4,000**	**5,000**	**6,000**
2	Analog	Sci Fi	Pro	0.08	0.08	0.08	0.08	0.08
3	Abyss & Apex	Fantasy & Sci Fi	Pro	0.05	$ 75.00	$ 75.00	$ 75.00	$ 75.00

Second Half:

	I	J	K	L	M	N	O	P
1	**7,000**	**7,500**	**8,000**	**9,000**	**10,000**	**10,000+**	**Notes**	**Guidelines**
2	0.08	0.08	$525	$600	$675	0.07	Prefer 2K-7K for shorts, 10K-20K for novelettes	Stories in which some aspect of future science or technology is so integral to the plot that, if that aspect were removed, the story would collapse. The science can be physical, sociological, psychological. The technology can be anything from electronic engineering to biogenetic engineering. But the stories must be strong and realistic, with believable people (who needn't be human) doing believable things–no matter how fantastic the background might be.
3	$ 75.00	$ 75.00	$ 75.00	$ 75.00	$ 75.00	$ 75.00	Up to 10K, prefer under 1,500	

Combined:

Name	Genre	Pay Rate	1,500	2,500	4,000	5,000	6,000	7,000	7,500	8,000	9,000	10,000	10,000+	Notes	Guidelines
Analog	Sci Fi	Pro	0.08	0.08	0.08	0.08	0.08	0.08	0.08	$525	$600	$675	0.07	Prefer 2K-7K for shorts, 10K-20K for novelettes	Stories in which some aspect of future science or technology is so integral to the plot that, if that aspect were removed, the story would collapse. The science can be physical, sociological, psychological. The technology can be anything from electronic engineering to biogenetic engineering. But the stories must be strong and realistic, with believable people (who needn't be human) doing believable things–no matter how fantastic the background might be.
Abyss & Apex	Fantasy & Sci Fi	Pro	0.05	$ 75.00	$ 75.00	$ 75.00	$ 75.00	$ 75.00	$ 75.00	$ 75.00	$ 75.00	$ 75.00	$ 75.00	Up to 10K, prefer under 1,500	
Apex	Fantasy & Sci Fi	Pro	0.05	0.05	0.05	0.05	N/A	N/A	N/A	N/A	N/A	N/A	N/A	Max 5K	We do not want hackneyed, cliched plots or neat, tidy stories that take no risks. We do not want Idea Stories without character development or prose style, nor do we want derivative fantasy with Tolkien's serial numbers filed off. What we want is sheer, unvarnished awesomeness. We want the stories it scared you to write. We want stories full of marrow and passion, stories that are twisted, strange, and beautiful. We want science fiction, fantasy, horror, and mash-ups of all three—the dark, weird stuff down at the bottom of your little literary heart.
Arc	Sci Fi	Pro	N/A	N/A	N/A	N/A	$2,370.00	$2,370.00	$2,370.00	$2,370.00	$2,370.00	$2,370.00	$2,370.00	Over 5K	We like technology and science, but we love people. The stories we're looking for will explore their anxieties, their joys and fears. We don't publish fantasy and if you send us anything with even a whiff of steampunk about it we will come round and burn down your house.

You'll see that it lists the market name and genre and whether the market is pro-paying or not (over 6 cents per word at the time) first. It then lists what that market pays at various popular word count levels.

You can see in the screenshot that some markets had flat rates above or below certain lengths, for example, and were only paying pro rates within a narrow word count range.

Finally, I included any notes about their stated length preferences and I copied and pasted in their guidelines. This put all the key information I needed in one place.

It was easy enough to build. Let's do it, shall we?

1. Label Cells A1:P1. (Name, Genre, Pay Rate, 1500, 2500, 4000, 5000, 6000, 7000, 7500, 8000, 9000, 10000, 10000+, Notes, Guidelines)
2. Bold the text in Cells A1:P1 and change the cell color using Fill Color.
3. Place a Border around all cells in columns A through P for as many rows as you think you'll need and middle align the text in those cells using Cell Text Alignment. Also Wrap Text for those cells.
4. Input your information for each market. For any market that pays a fixed rate, change the cell formatting using Currency Formatting.

That's it. No formulas. Just a simple listing of information. But one you can later filter to find the markets that meet your criteria.

Short Story Submissions Grid

Alright. Now that we've covered how to track your short stories and potential markets, it's time for the beautiful masterpiece I used to use to track my short story submissions. I'd regularly print this grid and keep a copy visible on my wall so I could see at a glance how I was doing and what stories were outstanding where. Warning, this is probably a bit over the top, but I loved it. It has formulas and color-coding and made me feel all warm and fuzzy every time I saw all those green cells and stars.

Okay, enough hype. Here it is:

	A	B	C	D	E	F	G	H	I	J	K	L	M	N
2		Story 1 (Wordcount)	Story 2 (Wordcount)	Story 3 (Wordcount)	Story 4 (Wordcount)			Personals	Form	Percent Personals	Asked to Submit More?		Mkt Average for Personals (Grinder)	Mkt Average Acceptance Rate (Grinder)
3	Market 1							0	0	0%			14%	4.0%
4	Market 2			★				1	0	100%			13%	2.2%
5	Market 3							0	0	0%	Yes		4%	0.0%
6	Market 4	×						0	1	0%	Form Yes		21%	2.0%
7	Market 5	×		★				1	1	50%	Form Yes		1%	1.8%
8	Market 6							0	0	0%	Form Yes			
9	Market 7			×	★			1	1	50%	Form Yes		6%	1.4%
10	Market 8	×			×			0	2	0%			11%	9.3%
11	Market 9			★				1	0	100%			28%	1.5%
12								4	5	44%				
13	Personal	0	0	3	1	4								
14	Form	3	0	1	1	5								
15	Total	3	0	4	2	9								
16	Percentage Personals	0%	0%	75%	50%	44%								

There's a lot going on here. Let's walk through it before we try to build it.

In Column A we have a listing of the different short story markets you've submitted to. In Row 2 we have each of the short stories you've completed with their word count shown in parens at the end of the title.

The cells where those two pieces of information intersect show the results of a submission for that story to that market.

If the cell is gray, that means that the short story isn't eligible to be submitted to that market. Maybe it's the wrong length or the wrong genre, for example.

If the cell is yellow that means the story has been submitted to that market, but a response is pending.

If the cell has a star in it, that means the story received a personal rejection.

If the cell has an x in it, that means the story received a form rejection.

If the cell is green, that means the rejection was positive in some way. If it's red, that means the rejection was not positive. As you can see, it's possible to get a personal rejection that's considered negative. I once received a personal rejection where the editor told me they absolutely hated my main character. Yay for me for making them hate my character? But I flagged that as a negative personal rejection. It wasn't an "I almost bought this…" rejection. It was a "Get this thing away from me…" rejection.

(You don't have to get this fancy. It's quite possible that the color-coding and exes and stars that I used doesn't work for you, which is fine. Use what will work for you. This is just one way to do it.)

Let's continue, though, because there's more.

In the sample, you can see that Rows 13 through 16 provide statistics on the number of personal versus form rejections for each story, and that Columns H through J do the same for each market.

Columns K, M, and N provide further supporting information related to the markets.

In Column J the markets where the percentage of personal rejections is higher than the market average are color-coded green.

And, lastly, in Cells F13:F16 there are summary statistics about the number of personals and form rejections across all stories and all markets, which matches the numbers in Cells H12:J12.

Ready to build this thing? It's going to be a lot of work, but it'll be fun, too. (Or is that just me?)

We're just going to do four short stories and nine markets like in the sample, but you should be able to expand it easily enough for however many stories and markets you want to track. Let's go:

1. In Cells B2:E2 add your short story names and word counts.
2. In Cells A3:A11 add your short story markets.
3. Label Cells A13:A16 and H2:K2 and M2:N2 with the appropriate labels. (Personal, Form, Total, Percent Personals, Personals, Form, Percent Personals, Asked to Submit More?, Mkt Average Personals, Mkt Average Acceptance Rate)
4. Change the Cell Text Orientation for Row 2 to 90 degrees.

5. Place Borders around Cells A2:E11, H2:K12, M2:N11, and A13:F16.
6. Use Fill Color to change the color of the cells between B3:E11 to gray if the short story in that column can't be submitted to the market in that row.
7. Use Fill Color to change the color of the cells between B3:E11 to yellow if the short story in that column is on submission to the market in that row.
8. Use Fill Color to change the color of the cells between B3:E11 to green if the short story in that column was already submitted to the market in that row and received a positive response. (A good personal or a "send more" comment.)
9. Use Fill Color to change the color of the cells between B3:E11 to red if the short story in that column was already submitted to the market in that row and received a negative or form response. (A negative personal or a form rejection with no request to send more.)
10. For any personal received, place a star in the cell. For any form rejection received, place an x in the cell. In my version of this worksheet, this was done using « and changing the font to Wingdings for the star and Ñ and changing the font to Wingdings 2 for the x.

(The easiest way to do this is to choose the Symbol from the Insert tab and then just copy it to other cells when you need it.)

11. In Cell B13 place the following formula: =COUNTIF(B3:B11,"«") where what is in the quotation marks is the textual representation of your symbol for a personal rejection.
12. In Cell B14 place the following formula: =COUNTIF(B3:B11,"Ñ") where what is in the quotation marks is the textual representation of your symbol for a form rejection.
13. In Cell B15 place the following formula: =B14+B13
14. In Cell B16 place the following formula: =IF(B13+B14=0,0,(B13/(B13+B14)))
15. Copy the formulas in Cells B13:B16 to Cells C13:E16.
16. In Cell F13 place the following formula: =SUM(B13:E13)
17. In Cell F14 place the following formula: =SUM(B14:E14)
18. In Cell F15 place the following formula: =F14+F13
19. In Cell F16 place the following formula: =IF(F13+F14=0,0,(F13/(F13+F14)))
20. In Cell H3 place the following formula: =COUNTIF(B3:E3,"«") where what is in the quotation marks is the textual representation of your symbol for a personal rejection.
21. In Cell I3 place the following formula: =COUNTIF(B3:E3,"Ñ") where what is in the quotation marks is the textual representation of your symbol for a form rejection.

22. In Cell J3 place the following formula: =IF(H3+I3=0,0,(H3/(H3+I3)))
23. Copy the formulas from Cells H3:J3 into Cells H4:J11
24. In Cell H12 place the following formula: =SUM(H3:H11)
25. In Cell I12 place the following formula: =SUM(I3:I11)
26. In Cell J12 place the following formula: =IF(H12+I12=0,0,(H12/(H12+I12)))
27. Almost there…If you had a "submit more" rejection from a market, note that in Column K.
28. Input the average percentage of personal rejections for each market as well as the average acceptance rate for each market into Columns M and N using The Submission Grinder's statistics.
29. Use Percent Formatting to format the values in Columns J, M, and N as well as Row 16.
30. And, last, but not least, apply Conditional Formatting to the values in Column J so that they're highlighted in green and the text is colored green if the percent of rejections that are personals is greater than the average listed in Column M.

(To do this, click into Cell J3 and go to Conditional Formatting under Styles on the Home tab. Choose Highlight Cell Rules from the dropdown menu and select Greater Than. Replace the 0% in the box with M3 and change the fill option to Green Fill with Dark Green Text. Once that's done, use the Format Painter to copy the conditional formatting to the rest of the cells in Column J.)

Phew. Glad we're done with that. But just think how cool it will be when Column J is completely green because every market you submit to loves your work and when you have a grid full of green stars from all those "almost there" rejections. Trust me, it might be the little thing that keeps you going through those dark moments when you wonder why you're doing this instead of sitting on your couch eating bonbons and watching *Real House Wives of Some Random City* or the appropriate sporting event of the season.

Okay. What next? It has to be easier than this one, right?

Right.

Let's turn our attention to novels.

Chapter and Scene Analysis

My first novel had three main viewpoints, three secondary viewpoints, and a few other one-off viewpoints. (Not recommended for a first novel.) With a novel like that you have to make sure you have the proper balance between the different viewpoints so that the story progresses and no one forgets a character and everyone is moving forward at the same pace.

Well, at least that's what I as a reader think should happen. It doesn't always.

In order to assist myself with this, I came up with a few different ways to analyze my chapters and scenes.

There are no hard and fast rules about how long a chapter should be or how much page time one viewpoint character should get compared to another, but I have a few "rules" I like to apply.

First, if I'm going to have more than one main character, I want each main character to get equal page time early on and to keep getting a steady amount of page time throughout the novel. That doesn't mean my chapters have to go in order from Character A to Character B to Character C and back to Character A throughout the book. But they can't go Character A, Character A, Character A, Character B, Character A, Character A, Character A, Character A, oh yeah, Character C.

Second, although I write short chapters in general, I like the shortest chapters to occur when the action picks up. This gives a subtle signal to the reader that we don't have time for debates about economics or descriptions of the pretty sunset right now because OH MY GOD big things are happening NOW.

Third, unless I'm deliberately writing a novel that involves two timelines I want all of the action from a specific week or day to be presented within a narrow set of chapters. (If the book hadn't been so heavy, there was one that I as a reader would've thrown across the room when I realized that two of the main viewpoint characters were experiencing events that were months apart. Something that was not obvious for a good couple hundred pages.)

Those are my rules. What I did may work for you, it may not. Hopefully if it doesn't work for you, you can at least see how to change things so it will.

Without further ado, here's the chapter and scene analysis I put together for my first novel with character names converted to just their first initial:

	A	B	C	D	E
1					
2	First Draft				
3	Chapter	Words			
4	1	2,027	G		
5	2	1,617	K		
6	3	1,878	G		
7	4	1,007	R		
8	5	1,244	G		
9	6	460	Narrator		
10	7	1,106	G		

What exactly are we looking at here? Well…

There's one row per chapter with a column for what chapter number it is, a column for the total word count for that chapter, and then a color-coded grid that takes up the next three columns.

I assigned each viewpoint a color. So main character "G" is green, main character "K" is light blue, and the third main character "R" is dark blue. Secondary character "L" is purple and other secondary character "M" is dark pink and then all other miscellaneous points of view are beige.

For chapters that have more than one scene and from more than one viewpoint, the columns can be used to show that. So in Chapter 8 of the first draft both K and R were present and each had a viewpoint scene within the chapter.

I could've instead colored this to show who was present in each chapter since at times the characters traveled together but the chapter was only from one of the viewpoints. Really, it comes down to what matters to you. Is it more important to know who was present or to know whose perspective is dominating the narrative? Or maybe both matter.

If they do, you could list in text which of the main characters are present. Or you could do a side-by-side grid to show in one who is present and in the other who is "telling" the story by being the viewpoint character. That approach could actually be very illuminating if you have a tendency to neglect a certain type of character.

* * *

Another approach you could take is to list each scene separately. Like this:

Full View:

Chapter/Scene	POV	Other Character 1	Other Character 2	Other Character 3	Other Character 4	Other Characters	Location	What happens	Word Count
1/1	R	K					ABC	DEF	750
1/2	R	G					GHI	JKL	852
2/1									

First Half:

	A	B	C	D	E	F
1	Chapter/Scene	POV	Other Character 1	Other Character 2	Other Character 3	Other Character 4
2	1/1	R	K			
3	1/2	R	G			
4	2/1					
5						

Second Half:

	G	H	I	J
1	Other Characters	Location	What happens	Word Count
2		ABC	DEF	750
3		GHI	JKL	852
4				
5				

This worksheet contains more information than the first example. In Column A it lists the chapter and then the scene within the chapter. Column B lists the point of view character for the scene. (I'm fine with shifting point of view between scenes within a chapter, but never within a scene.) Columns C through G would list the other main characters that are present in the scene. Column H lists where the scene takes place, Column I lists what happens, and Column J lists the word count for the scene. This pretty much summarizes all the key information you need to know about each scene in your average novel.

In this particular novel there was a set of moral precepts that were central to how the characters lived their lives, so I actually had a couple of additional columns where I tracked whether those were mentioned and what was said when they were. One, it let me know what had been set forth as the particular religion of the place and two, it let me make sure that they were mentioned often enough to serve their purpose.

What you track is only limited by your interest and willingness to do so.

* * *

A third way I approached this novel was by creating a timeline view.

One of the issues I had with the first draft was that too much happened for one of the characters at the start, which threw off the balance that was supposed to exist between all three of the viewpoints.

So I came up with this to visualize what my gut was telling me was wrong:

	A	B	C	D	E	F
1		**Week 1**		**Week 2**		**We**
2		**First Half**	**Second Half**	**First Half**	**Second Half**	**First Half**
3	**G**	What Happens (1)	What Happens (3)		What Happens (5)	
4	**K**	What Happens (2)				
5	**R**			What Happens (4)		
6	**L**					
7	**Other**					What Happens (6)

It shows the timeline across the top and lists each of the major viewpoint characters on the left side. A description of each chapter is listed at the intersection of those two points for each character in the scene. The description includes the chapter number as well to make sure that the timeline is kept together, although you'll notice any timeline skips when you're putting the information into your grid.

For me it let me see how one of the characters was dominating too much of the early timeline in the first draft.

* * *

So there you have it.

Three different ways of showing and visualizing your chapter and scene information to help you analyze what you've written. It may work for you, it may not.

We aren't going to build them because there's not much to build and what you build will very much depend on what you want to analyze and how your novel is structured. Your novel could take place over the course of one day, one week, one month, one year, or one century. And it could have one viewpoint character or be omniscient for all I know. So what moving parts you need to track and how will be different from what I needed to track. But hopefully this gave you a few ideas of how you could approach it using Excel. (I also sometimes just get out the white board and some markers, too, when I'm trying to see if I have the story arc right. Whatever works.)

Tracking Character Names

Before we wrap this up, let's add one last very simple type of information tracking that you might need to consider. Tracking character names. This is very, very simple, but very helpful, too.

I have a series of short stories I publish where the theme stays the same but the characters change. What I found after the first handful of stories is that I was tempted to repeat character names. John is such an easy, go-to name for a contemporary character, for example.

Take each story on its own and who cares. But ideally people will like your writing enough to read more of it. And to binge read it all at once. So those half a dozen stories you wrote over the course of a year may be read in two days. And I can guarantee that when that happens, readers will notice repeating character names. And not be happy.

So how do you keep track so you don't repeat yourself?

With Excel, of course.

What I used for my short story collection was this:

	A	B	C	D	E
1	Story	Main Character 1	Main Character 2	Secondary Character 1	Secondary Character 2
2					
3					
4					
5					
6					

It lists the story name, the main character name, the other main character name, and the secondary character names. That's it. Just a simple listing of information in a location you can reference easily.

You could list the title, the character name, and their purpose or role just as easily. Whatever you have to do to avoid repeating yourself. (Hair colors and eye colors might be another good thing to list, too, so you don't end up with all of your heroes being dark-haired and blue-eyed and all of your heroines being red-haired with green eyes....)

Conclusion

So there you have it. Various ways in which you can use Excel to track or support your writing. I hope you don't just stop there. Instead, think about what you want to track and how you could do so with something like Excel. You'll be amazed at all the possibilities and how it can really make your life easier.

(Okay, so maybe that's just the nerd that used to do interest calculations in the margins of my class notes talking.) But, really, the uses of Excel are unlimited. And I hope that this book has given you just a little bit of insight into some of your options.

If you do come up with a new idea but are struggling on how to implement it, drop me a line: mlhumphreywriter@gmail.com. I'd be happy to help you figure it out. Same with if you have any questions about what's in this book. I don't check that account every day, but I will get back to you.

Good luck with it!

(And if you find yourself self-publishing at some point you might want to check out *Data Analysis for Self-Publishers*. Or if you want to explore more about selling what you write, check out *Sell That Book*.)

And don't forget, the appendices have a brief overview of each technique used in this guide.

Appendix A: Inputting Information and Navigating Excel

Add Columns

To add a column to your worksheet, right-click on the column where you want your new column to be and select Insert from the dropdown menu. Or you can highlight the column where you want your new column to be, go to the Cells section of the Home tab, and click on Insert and then choose Insert Sheet Columns.

Auto Fill

Auto Fill leverages Excel's ability to identify patterns and repeat them for you so you don't have to enter your complete data set. It works best with obvious patterns such as 1, 2, 3...; Monday, Tuesday, Wednesday…; or January, February, March…

To use Auto Fill, start your pattern, highlight the cells that contain the pattern you want to continue, click in the bottom right corner of the last cell, and drag either downward or to the right, whichever direction you want the pattern to continue.

Copying

To copy the contents of a cell(s), highlight what you want to copy, and use (1) Ctrl + C, (2) right-click and Copy, or (3) select Copy from the Clipboard section of the Home tab. Move to the new location and Paste.

Remember that when you copy a cell that contains a formula that the formula will adjust when moved and will no longer reference the same cells. If you need the cell references to remain the same, use a $ in front of the column and row references.

Cutting

To cut and move the contents of a cell, highlight what you want to cut, and use (1) Ctrl + X, (2) right-click and Cut, or (3) select Cut from the Clipboard section of the Home tab. To place those contents in a new location, use Paste.

When you cut and move a cell that contains a formula, the formula will remain the exact same as it was in the original cell.

Freeze Panes

If you want to be able to see the top row(s) of your worksheet or the left-most column(s) of your worksheet no matter where you are in the worksheet, then you want to use Freeze Panes. To freeze panes, click into the cell just below the rows you want to keep visible and just to the right of the columns you want to keep visible. Go to the View tab and choose Freeze Panes from the Freeze Panes dropdown menu.

Insert Rows

To insert a row into your worksheet, right-click on the row where you want your new row to be, and choose Insert from the dropdown menu. You can also go to the Cells section of the Home tab and choose Insert Sheet Rows from the Insert dropdown.

Insert Symbols

You can insert a symbol into a cell with existing text or into its own cell. To insert a symbol, go to the Symbols section of the Insert tab and click on the Symbol icon. This will bring up a number of choices. If you see what you want, click on it, and then choose Insert. If you don't see what you want, try changing the font from normal text to one of the Wingdings fonts which will give you more options.

When you insert a symbol it will show in the formula bar as a character, like [, but will display as the symbol you choose. If you change the font, the symbol will not display correctly anymore.

Pasting

Once you have copied or cut an item, to paste it into a new location, use (1) Ctrl + V, (2) right-click and Paste, or (3) select Paste from the Clipboard section of the Home tab.

Use Paste Special to paste just values or to transpose the content.

Appendix B: Formatting

Bolding Text

To bold text, highlight the selected text or cell(s) and use (1) Ctrl + B, (2) click on the B in the Font section of the Home tab, or (3) right-click, choose Format Cells, go to the Font tab, and change the Font Style to Bold.

Borders

To place a border around a cell or cells, highlight the selected cells, and (1) click on the border dropdown in the Font section of the Home tab or (2) right-click, choose Format Cells, go to the Border tab, and choose the border you want to add.

> *Remember that if you want to change the color or the line type of the border from the default, do so before you choose your borders.*

Cell Text Alignment

To change the alignment of the text within a cell or cells, highlight the cell(s), and then (1) in the Alignment section on the Home tab select the type of desired cell alignments (Top Align, Middle Align, Bottom Align and Align Left, Center, Align Right) or (2) right-click, choose Format Cells, go to the Alignment tab, and choose the desired Horizontal and Vertical alignment types from the dropdown menus.

Cell Text Orientation

To change the orientation of the text within a cell, highlight the cell(s), and then (1) in the Alignment section on the Home tab, choose your type of desired orientation from the orientation dropdown menu or (2) right-click, choose Format Cells, go to the Alignment Tab, and change the orientation from 0 degrees to the desired orientation by either clicking and dragging the orientation line or inputting your desired value in the Degrees field.

Column Width

To adjust the width of a column, (1) click on the right-hand side at the top of the column and drag to the desired width, (2) double-click on the right-hand side at the top of the column to auto-adjust the width, or (3) select the column, right-click, choose Column Width, and enter a new width for the column.

Currency Formatting

To format a cell as currency, select the cell(s) and (1) click on the $ sign in the Number section of the Home tab, (2) select Currency or Accounting from the dropdown menu in the Number section of the Home tab, or (3) right-click, choose Format Cells, go to the Number tab, and choose Currency or Accounting from the available list.

Date Formatting

To format a cell as a date, select the cell(s) and (1) select Short Date or Long Date from the dropdown menu in the Number section of the Home tab, or (2) right-click, choose Format Cells, go to the Number tab, and choose Date from the available list and then choose a date type from the box of examples.

Fill Color

To fill a cell with a specific color, select the cell(s) and (1) choose the color from the Fill Color dropdown menu in the Font section of the Home tab, or (2) right-click, choose Format Cells, go to the Fill tab, and choose a color.

Italicizing Text

To italicize text, highlight the selected text or cell(s) and use (1) Ctrl + I, (2) click on the I in the Font section of the Home tab, or (3) right-click, choose Format Cells, go to the Font tab, and change the Font Style to Italic.

Merge and Center

To merge a selection of cells and center your selected text across those cells, make sure the text you want to keep is in the top left-most cell of the selection, highlight the cells you want to merge, and click on Merge & Center in the Alignment section of the Home tab.

Number Formatting

To format a cell as a number, select the cell(s) and (1) click on the comma sign in the Number section of the Home tab, (2) select Number from the dropdown menu in the Number section of the Home tab, or (3) right-click, choose Format Cells, go to the Number tab, and choose Number from the available list. You can set the desired number of decimal places either in the Number section of the Home tab (using the 0.00 images with arrows next to them) or in the Format Cells dialogue box once you've chosen Number as your format type.

Percent Formatting

To format a cell as a percentage, select the cell(s) and (1) click on the % sign in the Number section of the Home tab, (2) select Percentage from the dropdown menu in the Number section of the Home tab, or (3) right-click, choose Format Cells, go to the Number tab, and choose Percentage from the available list.

Row Height

To adjust the height of a row, (1) click on the bottom edge of the row name and drag to the desired height, (2) double-click on the bottom edge of the row name to auto-adjust the height, or (3) right-click on the row name, choose Row Height, and enter a new height for the row.

Underlining Text

To underline text, highlight the selected text or cell(s) and use (1) Ctrl + U, (2) click on the U in the Font section of the Home tab, or (3) right-click, choose Format Cells, go to the Font tab, and change the Underline dropdown menu to the chosen type of underline.

Wrap Text

To wrap the text within a cell so that it flows onto multiple lines within the cell based upon the cell's width, highlight the cell(s) and (1) click on Wrap Text in the Alignment section of the Home tab, or (2) right-click, choose Format Cells, go to the Alignment tab, and check the Wrap text box.

Appendix C: Math, Analysis, and Using Formulas

AutoSum

The AutoSum function is a convenient way to add values that are in a column or row. Click into the cell after the last value you want to sum and then go to the Editing section of the Home tab and click on the AutoSum option. It will provide a SUM formula that includes all values above or to the left of the cell up to the next blank space.

Addition

You can perform simple addition using the + sign or sum multiple values using the SUM ( ) function. For example =A1+B2 will add cells A1 and B2 together. Or =SUM(A1:A25) will sum cells A1 through A25.

Complex Formulas

Excel allows for complex formulas where more than one function is completed within a cell. When using complex formulas, be sure that you use parens properly because =A1+B2/C1 is different from =(A1+B2)/C1.

Conditional Formatting

Conditional formatting allows you to specify formatting for a cell or range of cells that will apply only when certain criteria are met. For example, you can have a cell turn red if the value falls below a certain threshold or green if it reaches a certain point. To apply conditional formatting, highlight the cell(s), go to the Styles section of the Home tab, and choose from the Conditional Formatting dropdown menu. In the example in this guide, the Highlight Cells Rules option was used.

COUNTIF Function

You can use the COUNTIF function to count the number of cells in the selected range that meet a specific criteria. For example, =COUNTIF(B3:B11,"«") looks at all of the cells between B3 and B11 and counts any of the cells where the value of the cell is «.

A more advanced version of the COUNTIF function is the COUNTIFS function which counts how many entries meet more than one criteria. So, for example, =COUNTIFS(D90:D94,"USD",B90:B94,">5") would count all entries in rows 90 through 94 where the value in Column D was USD and the value in Column B was greater than 5.

Division

You can perform division using the / sign. For example, =A1/B2 will divide A1 by B2.

Filtering

If you have your data arranged with a header row and then the information listed in rows below that, you can filter your data to look at just those rows of data that meet certain criteria. To do so, click into the header row and choose Filter from the Sort & Filter dropdown in the Editing section of the Home tab. The filter will only work for contiguous columns. (So if you have a blank column in the middle of your header row, it will only allow filtering on columns to the left of the blank column or to the right of the blank column, but not on both at once.)

To choose your filter criteria, click on the arrow next to the column header. You can filter by using the checkboxes next to each listed value, by applying filtering criteria such as equals or contains, or by text or highlight color.

Holding a Cell Reference Constant When Copying a Formula

If you want to copy a formula but want to keep the reference to a cell constant, then you need to use the $ sign. For example, if you have a formula =(A3+B3)/C1 and you want to copy that formula so that the references to A3 and B3 change to reflect the row they're in, but keep the reference to Cell C1 constant, then you would write the formula as =(A3+B3)/$C$1. If you want to just keep the column reference constant, only put the $ sign in front of the letter portion of the cell reference ($C1). If you want to just keep the row reference constant, only put the $ sign in front of the number portion of the cell reference (C$1).

IF Function

You can use the IF( ) function to create an either/or scenario where if one criteria is met, result A is returned, and if not, result B is returned. So, for example, =IF(B3=0," ",B2/B3) says that if cell B3 is equal to zero, then leave the cell blank, otherwise divide cell B2 by cell B3.

Note that you don't need to use an equals sign for the formulas that are performed under each scenario.

If you want to be more complex, you can create nested IF( ) functions that have more than two possible outcomes. For example, =IF(B3=0," ",IF(B3>10,B3*3,B3)) is a formula that says that if B3 equals zero then return a blank value, if instead it's greater than ten, then return a value that's equal to B3 times 3, and if neither of those criteria are met, then return a value equal to B3.

There is a limit on how many IF functions you can nest. According to my current version of Excel that number is 64, but in earlier versions of Excel it was much lower. (According to my search results, it was 7 previously.)

MAX Function

The MAX( ) function allows you to determine the maximum value from a selected group of cells. For example =MAX(A1:B25) would give you the maximum value in cells A1 through B25.

Multiplication

You can perform simple multiplication using the * sign or multiply many values using the PRODUCT( ) function. For example, =A1*B2 will multiply Cell A1 by Cell B2. Or =PRODUCT(A1:A25) will multiply Cell A1 by Cell A2 by Cell A3 through to Cell A25.

Pivot Tables

Pivot Tables allow you to summarize information from a table and to calculate the intersection of multiple variables from a table of data. To build a pivot table, select the header row and rows of data that you want to analyze, and then go to the Insert tab and choose Pivot Table from the Tables section.

You can drag your chosen variables to either the table itself or to the display in the bottom right corner.

Be sure that the variables in the Values section are returning the type of result you want. Mine often defaults to count when I would prefer sum. This can be changed by clicking on the arrow and selecting Value Field Settings.

You can have multiple variables in your Rows or Columns.

You can filter your results by placing a variable in the Filters section of the table. (By, for example, year or vendor or market or project.)

You don't have to have both a column and a row, you can have one or the other and then use the values section to specify what you want to summarize.

Subtraction

You can perform subtraction using the - sign. For example, =A1-B2 will subtract B2 from A1.

TEXT Function

The TEXT( ) function is very interesting. It doesn't just convert something to text. In the case where it was used here, we used it to convert a date to the date's day of the week in text format using =TEXT(A1,"dddd") as our formula. This function allows you to display components of a date as numbers, abbreviations, or full text. It also allows for very specific formatting of numbers and times. See Excel's help for the TEXT function to see all the available options.

WEEKNUM Function

The WEEKNUM( ) function returns the number of the week, 1 through 53, in the year that a specified date falls on. It's useful for when you want to summarize data on a weekly basis or, as used here, create a grid of results by week and day of the week. The default is to assume that the week containing January 1 is the first week of the year and that the week begins on a Sunday.

About the Author

M.L. Humphrey is a former stockbroker with a degree in Economics from Stanford and an MBA from Wharton who has spent over twenty-five years as a regulator, consultant, and fraud investigator in the finance industry.

You can reach M.L. at mlhumphreywriter@gmail.com or at mlhumphrey.com.

* * *

To buy ebook titles direct go to https://payhip.com/mlhumphrey.

For Excel templates go to https://payhip.com/mlhumphrey/collection/excel-templates

www.ingramcontent.com/pod-product-compliance
Lightning Source LLC
LaVergne TN
LVHW080000210926
848481LV00012B/3635
* 9 7 8 1 9 5 0 9 0 2 4 1 5 *